Sixty Poems

Sixty Poems

Charles Simic

A HARVEST ORIGINAL
HARCOURT, INC.
Orlando ★ Austin ★ New York ★ San Diego ★ London

To Helen

www.HarcourtBooks.com

Library of Congress Cataloging-in-Publication Data
Simic, Charles, 1938–
[Poems. Selections.]
Sixty poems/Charles Simic.—1st ed.
p. cm.
"A Harvest book."
I. Title. II. Title: 60 poems.
PS3569.I4725A6 2008
811'.54—dc22 2007035942
ISBN 978-0-15-603564-4

Text set in Dante
Designed by Scott Piehl

Printed in the United States of America
First edition
C E G I K J H F D B

CONTENTS

From *Unending Blues*, 1986

TOWARD NIGHTFALL

for Don and Jane

The weight of tragic events
On everyone's back,
Just as tragedy
In the proper Greek sense
Was thought impossible
To compose in our day.

There were scaffolds,
Makeshift stages,
Puny figures on them,
Like small indistinct animals
Caught in the headlights
Crossing the road way ahead,

In the gray twilight
That went on hesitating
On the verge of a huge
Starless autumn night.
One could've been in
The back of an open truck
Hunkering because of
The speed and chill.

One could've been walking
With a sidelong glance
At the many troubling shapes
The bare trees made—
Like those about to shriek,

But finding themselves unable
To utter a word now.

One could've been in
One of these dying mill towns
Inside a small dim grocery
When the news broke.
One would've drawn near the radio
With the one many months pregnant
Who serves there at that hour.

Was there a smell of
Spilled blood in the air,
Or was it that other,
Much finer scent—of fear,
The fear of approaching death
One met on the empty street?

Monsters on movie posters, too,
Prominently displayed.
Then, six factory girls,
Arm in arm, laughing
As if they've been drinking.
At the very least, one
Could've been one of them:

The one with a mouth
Painted bright red,
Who feels out of sorts,
For no reason, very pale,
And so, excusing herself,
Vanishes where it says:
Rooms for Rent,

And immediately goes to bed,
Fully dressed, only

To lie with eyes open,
Trembling, despite the covers.
It's just a bad chill,
She keeps telling herself
Not having seen the papers
Which the landlord has the dog
Bring from the front porch.

The old man never learned
To read well, and so
Reads on in that half-whisper,
And in that half-light
Verging on the dark,
About that day's tragedies
Which supposedly are not
Tragedies in the absence of
Figures endowed with
Classic nobility of soul.

AGAINST WHATEVER IT IS THAT'S ENCROACHING

Best of all is to be idle,
And especially on a Thursday,
And to sip wine while studying the light:
The way it ages, yellows, turns ashen
And then hesitates forever
On the threshold of the night
That could be bringing the first frost.

It's good to have a woman around just then,
And two is even better.
Let them whisper to each other
And eye you with a smirk.
Let them roll up their sleeves and unbutton their shirts a bit
As this fine old twilight deserves,

And the small schoolboy
Who has come home to a room almost dark
And now watches wide-eyed
The grown-ups raise their glasses to him,
The giddy-headed, red-haired woman
With eyes tightly shut,
As if she were about to cry or sing.

From *The Book of Gods and Devils,* 1990

ST. THOMAS AQUINAS

I left parts of myself everywhere
The way absent-minded people leave
Gloves and umbrellas
Whose colors are sad from dispensing so much bad luck.

I was on a park bench asleep.
It was like the Art of Ancient Egypt.
I didn't wish to bestir myself.
I made my long shadow take the evening train.

"We give death to a child when we give it a doll,"
Said the woman who had read Djuna Barnes.
We whispered all night. She had traveled to darkest Africa.
She had many stories to tell about the jungle.

I was already in New York looking for work.
It was raining as in the days of Noah.
I stood in many doorways of that great city.
Once I asked a man in a tuxedo for a cigarette.
He gave me a frightened look and stepped out into the rain.

Since "man naturally desires happiness,"
According to St. Thomas Aquinas,
Who gave irrefutable proof of God's existence and purpose,
I loaded trucks in the Garment Center.
A black man and I stole a woman's red dress.
It was of silk; it shimmered.

Upon a gloomy night with all our loving ardors on fire,
We carried it down the long empty avenue,
Each holding one sleeve.
The heat was intolerable causing many terrifying human faces
To come out of hiding.

In the Public Library Reading Room
There was a single ceiling fan barely turning.
I had the travels of Herman Melville to serve me as a pillow.
I was on a ghost ship with its sails fully raised.
I could see no land anywhere.
The sea and its monsters could not cool me.

I followed a saintly-looking nurse into a doctor's office.
We edged past people with eyes and ears bandaged.
"I am a medieval philosopher in exile,"
I explained to my landlady that night.
And, truly, I no longer looked like myself.
I wore glasses with a nasty spider crack over one eye.

I stayed in the movies all day long.
A woman on the screen walked through a bombed city
Again and again. She wore army boots.
Her legs were long and bare. It was cold wherever she was.
She had her back turned to me, but I was in love with her.
I expected to find wartime Europe at the exit.

It wasn't even snowing! Everyone I met
Wore a part of my destiny like a carnival mask.
"I'm Bartleby the Scrivener," I told the Italian waiter.
"Me, too," he replied.
And I could see nothing but overflowing ashtrays
The human-faced flies were busy examining.

FACTORY

The machines were gone, and so were those who worked them.
A single high-backed chair stood like a throne
In all that empty space.
I was on the floor making myself comfortable
For a long night of little sleep and much thinking.

An empty birdcage hung from a steam pipe.
In it I kept an apple and a small paring knife.
I placed newspapers all around me on the floor
So I could jump at the slightest rustle.
It was like the scratching of a pen,
The silence of the night writing in its diary.

Of rats who came to pay me a visit
I had the highest opinion.
They'd stand on two feet
As if about to make a polite request
On a matter of great importance.

Many other strange things came to pass.
Once a naked woman climbed on the chair
To reach the apple in the cage.
I was on the floor watching her go on tiptoe,
Her hand fluttering in the cage like a bird.

On other days, the sun peeked through dusty windowpanes
To see what time it was. But there was no clock,
Only the knife in the cage, glinting like a mirror,
And the chair in the far corner
Where someone once sat facing the brick wall.

SHELLEY

for M. Follain

Poet of the dead leaves driven like ghosts,
Driven like pestilence-stricken multitudes,
I read you first
One rainy evening in New York City,

In my atrocious Slavic accent,
Saying the mellifluous verses
From a battered, much-stained volume
I had bought earlier that day
In a secondhand bookstore on Fourth Avenue
Run by an initiate of the occult masters.

The little money I had being almost spent,
I walked the streets, my nose in the book.
I sat in a dingy coffee shop
With last summer's dead flies on the table.
The owner was an ex-sailor
Who had grown a huge hump on his back
While watching the rain, the empty street.
He was glad to have me sit and read,
He'd refill my cup with a liquid dark as river Styx.

Shelley spoke of a mad, blind, dying king;
Of rulers who neither see, nor feel, nor know;
Of graves from which a glorious Phantom may
Burst to illumine our tempestuous day.

I too felt like a glorious phantom
Going to have my dinner
In a Chinese restaurant I knew so well.
It had a three-fingered waiter
Who'd bring my soup and rice each night
Without ever saying a word.

I never saw anyone else there.
The kitchen was separated by a curtain
Of glass beads which clicked faintly
Whenever the front door opened.
The front door opened that evening
To admit a pale little girl with glasses.

The poet spoke of the everlasting universe
Of things ... of gleams of a remoter world
Which visit the soul in sleep ...
Of a desert peopled by storms alone ...

The streets were strewn with broken umbrellas
Which looked like funereal kites
This little Chinese girl might have made.
The bars on MacDougal Street were emptying.
There had been a fistfight.
A man leaned against a lamppost, arms extended as if crucified,
The rain washing the blood off his face.

In a dimly lit side street,
Where the sidewalk shone like a ballroom mirror
At closing time—

A well-dressed man without any shoes
Asked me for money.
His eyes shone, he looked triumphant
Like a fencing master
Who had just struck a mortal blow.

How strange it all was ... The world's raffle
That dark October night ...
The yellowed volume of poetry
With its Splendors and Glooms
Which I studied by the light of storefronts:
Drugstores and barbershops,
Afraid of my small windowless room
Cold as a tomb of an infant emperor.

THE DEVILS

You were a "victim of semiromantic anarchism
In its most irrational form."
I was "ill at ease in an ambiguous world

Deserted by Providence." We drank wine
And made love in the afternoon. The neighbors'
TVs were tuned to soap operas.

The unhappy couples spoke little.
There were interminable pauses.
Soft organ music. Someone coughing.

"It's like Strindberg's *Dream Play*," you said.
"What is?" I asked and got no reply.
I was watching a spider on the ceiling.

It was the kind St. Veronica ate in her martyrdom.
"That woman subsisted on spiders only,"
I told the janitor when he came to fix the faucet.

He wore dirty overalls and a derby hat.
Once he had been an inmate of a notorious state institution.
"I'm no longer Jesus," he informed us happily.

He believed only in devils now.
"This building is full of them," he confided.
One could see their horns and tails

If one caught them in their baths.
"He's got Dark Ages on his brain," you said.
"Who does?" I asked and got no reply.

The spider had the beginnings of a web
Over our heads. The world was quiet
Except when one of us took a sip of wine.

THE WHITE ROOM

The obvious is difficult
To prove. Many prefer
The hidden. I did, too.
I listened to the trees.

They had a secret
Which they were about to
Make known to me,
And then didn't.

Summer came. Each tree
On my street had its own
Scheherazade. My nights
Were a part of their wild

Storytelling. We were
Entering dark houses,
More and more dark houses
Hushed and abandoned.

There was someone with eyes closed
On the upper floors.
The thought of it, and the wonder,
Kept me sleepless.

The truth is bald and cold,
Said the woman
Who always wore white.
She didn't leave her room much.

The sun pointed to one or two
Things that had survived
The long night intact,
The simplest things,

Difficult in their obviousness.
They made no noise.
It was the kind of day
People describe as "perfect."

Gods disguising themselves
As black hairpins? A hand mirror?
A comb with a tooth missing?
No! That wasn't it.

Just things as they are,
Unblinking, lying mute
In that bright light,
And the trees waiting for the night.

THE BIG WAR

We played war during the war,
Margaret. Toy soldiers were in big demand,
The kind made from clay.
The lead ones they melted into bullets, I suppose.

You never saw anything as beautiful
As those clay regiments! I used to lie on the floor
For hours staring them in the eye.
I remember them staring back at me in wonder.

How strange they must have felt
Standing stiffly at attention
Before a large, incomprehending creature
With a moustache made of milk.

In time they broke, or I broke them on purpose.
There was wire inside their limbs,
Inside their chests, but nothing in the heads!
Margaret, I made sure.

Nothing at all in the heads . . .
Just an arm, now and then, an officer's arm,
Wielding a saber from a crack
In my deaf grandmother's kitchen floor.

PARADISE

In a neighborhood once called "Hell's Kitchen"
Where a beggar claimed to be playing Nero's fiddle
While the city burned in midsummer heat;
Where a lady barber who called herself Cleopatra
Wielded the scissors of fate over my head
Threatening to cut off my ears and nose;
Where a man and a woman went walking naked
In one of the dark side streets at dawn.

I must be dreaming, I told myself.
It was like meeting a couple of sphinxes.
I expected them to have wings, bodies of lions:
Him with his wildly tattooed chest;
Her with her huge, dangling breasts.

It happened so quickly, and so long ago!

You know that time just before the day breaks
When one yearns to lie down on cool sheets
In a room with shades drawn?
The hour when the beautiful suicides
Lying side by side in the morgue
Get up and walk out into the first light.

The curtains of cheap hotels flying out of windows
Like seagulls, but everything else quiet...
Steam rising out of the subway gratings...
Bodies glistening with sweat...
Madness, and you might even say, paradise!

IN THE LIBRARY

for Octavio

There's a book called
A Dictionary of Angels.
No one had opened it in fifty years,
I know, because when I did,
The covers creaked, the pages
Crumbled. There I discovered

The angels were once as plentiful
As species of flies.
The sky at dusk
Used to be thick with them.
You had to wave both arms
Just to keep them away.

Now the sun is shining
Through the tall windows.
The library is a quiet place.
Angels and gods huddled
In dark unopened books.
The great secret lies
On some shelf Miss Jones
Passes every day on her rounds.

She's very tall, so she keeps
Her head tipped as if listening.
The books are whispering.
I hear nothing, but she does.

From *Hotel Insomnia,* 1992

THE PRODIGAL

Dark morning rain
Meant to fall
On a prison and a school yard,
Falling meanwhile
On my mother and her old dog.

How slow she shuffles now
In my father's Sunday shoes.
The dog by her side
Trembling with each step
As he tries to keep up.

I am on another corner waiting
With my head shaved.
My mind hops like a sparrow
In the rain.
I'm always watching and worrying about her.

Everything is a magic ritual,
A secret cinema,
The way she appears in a window hours later
To set the empty bowl
And spoon on the table,
And then exits
So that the day may pass,
And the night may fall

Into the empty bowl,
Empty room, empty house,
While the rain keeps
Knocking at the front door.

HOTEL INSOMNIA

I liked my little hole,
Its window facing a brick wall.
Next door there was a piano.
A few evenings a month
A crippled old man came to play
"My Blue Heaven."

Mostly, though, it was quiet.
Each room with its spider in heavy overcoat
Catching his fly with a web
Of cigarette smoke and revery.
So dark,
I could not see my face in the shaving mirror.

At 5 A.M. the sound of bare feet upstairs.
The "Gypsy" fortune-teller,
Whose storefront is on the corner,
Going to pee after a night of love.
Once, too, the sound of a child sobbing.
So near it was, I thought
For a moment, I was sobbing myself.

THE TIGER

in memory of George Oppen

In San Francisco, that winter,
There was a dark little store
Full of sleepy Buddhas.
The afternoon I walked in,
No one came out to greet me.
I stood among the sages
As if trying to read their thoughts.

One was huge and made of stone.
A few were the size of a child's head
And had stains the color of dried blood.
There were some no bigger than mice,
And they appeared to be listening.

"The winds of March, black winds,
The gritty winds," the dead poet wrote.

At sundown his street was empty
Except for my long shadow
Open before me like scissors.
There was his house where I told the story
Of the Russian soldier,
The one who looked Chinese.

He lay wounded in my father's bed,
And I brought him water and matches.
For that he gave me a little tiger
Made of ivory. Its mouth was open in anger,
But it had no stripes left.

There was the night when I colored
Its eyes black, its tongue red.
My mother held the lamp for me,
While worrying about the kind of luck
This beast might bring us.

The tiger in my hand growled faintly
When we were alone in the dark,
But when I put my ear to the poet's door
That afternoon, I heard nothing.

"The winds of march, black winds,
The gritty winds," he once wrote.

A BOOK FULL OF PICTURES

Father studied theology through the mail
And this was exam time.
Mother knitted. I sat quietly with a book
Full of pictures. Night fell.
My hands grew cold touching the faces
Of dead kings and queens.

There was a black raincoat
    in the upstairs bedroom
Swaying from the ceiling,
But what was it doing there?
Mother's long needles made quick crosses.
They were black
Like the inside of my head just then.

The pages I turned sounded like wings.
"The soul is a bird," he once said.
In my book full of pictures
A battle raged: lances and swords
Made a kind of wintry forest
With my heart spiked and bleeding in its branches.

EVENING WALK

You give the appearance of listening
To my thoughts, O trees,
Bent over the road I am walking
On a late summer evening
When every one of you is a steep staircase
The night is slowly descending.

The high leaves like my mother's lips
Forever trembling, unable to decide,
For there's a bit of wind,
And it's like hearing voices,
Or a mouth full of muffled laughter,
A huge dark mouth we can all fit in
Suddenly covered by a hand.

Everything quiet. Light
Of some other evening strolling ahead,
Long-ago evening of silk dresses,
Bare feet, hair unpinned and falling.
Happy heart, what heavy steps you take
As you follow after them in the shadows.

The sky at the road's end cloudless and blue.
The night birds like children
Who won't come to dinner.
Lost children in the darkening woods.

ROMANTIC SONNET

Evenings of sovereign clarity—
Wine and bread on the table,
Mother praying,
Father naked in bed.

Was I that skinny boy stretched out
In the field behind the house,
His heart cut out with a toy knife?
Was I the crow hovering over him?

Happiness, you are the bright red lining
Of the dark winter coat
Grief wears inside out.

This is about myself when I'm remembering,
And your long insomniac's nails,
O Time, I keep chewing and chewing.

THE OLD WORLD

for Dan and Jeanne

I believe in the soul; so far
It hasn't made much difference.
I remember an afternoon in Sicily.
The ruins of some temple.
Columns fallen in the grass like naked lovers.

The olives and goat cheese tasted delicious
And so did the wine
With which I toasted the coming night,
The darting swallows,
The Saracen wind and moon.

It got darker. There was something
Long before there were words:
The evening meal of shepherds . . .
A fleeting whiteness among the trees . . .
Eternity eavesdropping on time.

The goddess going to bathe in the sea.
She must not be followed.
These rocks, these cypress trees,
May be her old lovers.
Oh to be one of them, the wine whispered to me.

COUNTRY FAIR

for Hayden Carruth

If you didn't see the six-legged dog,
It doesn't matter.
We did and he mostly lay in the corner.
As for the extra legs,

One got used to them quickly
And thought of other things.
Like, what a cold, dark night
To be out at the fair.

Then the keeper threw a stick
And the dog went after it
On four legs, the other two flapping behind,
Which made one girl shriek with laughter.

She was drunk and so was the man
Who kept kissing her neck.
The dog got the stick and looked back at us.
And that was the whole show.

From *A Wedding in Hell,* 1994

PARADISE MOTEL

Millions were dead; everybody was innocent.
I stayed in my room. The President
Spoke of war as of a magic love potion.
My eyes were opened in astonishment.
In a mirror my face appeared to me
Like a twice-canceled postage stamp.

I lived well, but life was awful.
There were so many soldiers that day,
So many refugees crowding the roads.
Naturally, they all vanished
With a touch of the hand.
History licked the corners of its bloody mouth.

On the pay channel, a man and a woman
Were trading hungry kisses and tearing off
Each other's clothes while I looked on
With the sound off and the room dark
Except for the screen where the color
Had too much red in it, too much pink.

THE CLOCKS OF THE DEAD

One night I went to keep the clock company.
It had a loud tick after midnight
As if it were uncommonly afraid.
It's like whistling past a graveyard,
I explained.
In any case, I told him I understood.

Once there were clocks like that
In every kitchen in America.
Now the factory's windows are all broken.
The old men on night shift are in Charon's boat.
The day you stop, I said to the clock,
The little wheels they keep in reserve
Will have rolled away
Into many hard-to-find places.

Just thinking about it, I forgot to wind the clock.
We woke up in the dark.
How quiet the city is, I said.
Like the clocks of the dead, my wife replied.
Grandmother on the wall,
I heard the snows of your childhood
Begin to fall.

LEAVES

Lovers who take pleasure
In the company of trees,
Who seek diversion after many kisses
In each other's arms,
Watching the leaves,

The way they quiver
At the slightest breath of wind,
The way they thrill,
And shudder almost individually,
One of them beginning to shake
While the others are still quiet,
Unaccountably, unreasonably—

What am I saying?
One leaf in a million more fearful,
More happy,
Than all the others?

On this oak tree casting
Such deep shade,
And my lids closing sleepily
With that one leaf twittering
Now darkly, now luminously.

TRANSPORT

In the frying pan
On the stove
I found my love
And me naked.

Chopped onions
Fell on our heads
And made us cry.
It's like a parade,
I told her, confetti
When some guy
Reaches the moon.

"Means of transport,"
She replied obscurely
While we fried.
"Means of transport!"

CRAZY ABOUT HER SHRIMP

We don't even take time
To come up for air.
We keep our mouths full and busy
Eating bread and cheese
And smooching in between.

No sooner have we made love
Than we are back in the kitchen.
While I chop the hot peppers,
She wiggles her ass
And stirs the shrimp on the stove.

How good the wine tastes
That has run red
Out of a laughing mouth!
Down her chin
And onto her naked tits.

"I'm getting fat," she says,
Turning this way and that way
Before the mirror.
"I'm crazy about her shrimp!"
I shout to the gods above.

READING HISTORY

for Hans Magnus

At times, reading here
In the library,
I'm given a glimpse
Of those condemned to death
Centuries ago,
And of their executioners.
I see each pale face before me
The way a judge
Pronouncing a sentence would,
Marveling at the thought
That I do not exist yet.

With eyes closed I can hear
The evening birds.
Soon they will be quiet
And the final night on earth
Will commence
In the fullness of its sorrow.

How vast, dark, and impenetrable
Are the early-morning skies
Of those led to their death
In a world from which I'm entirely absent,
Where I can still watch
Someone's slumped back,

Someone who is walking away from me
With his hands tied,
His graying head still on his shoulders,

Someone who
In what little remains of his life
Knows in some vague way about me,
And thinks of me as God,
As Devil.

EMPIRES

My grandmother prophesied the end
Of your empires, O fools!
She was ironing. The radio was on.
The earth trembled beneath our feet.

One of your heroes was giving a speech.
"Monster," she called him.
There were cheers and gun salutes for the monster.
"I could kill him with my bare hands,"
She announced to me.

There was no need to. They were all
Going to the devil any day now.
"Don't go blabbering about this to anyone,"
She warned me.
And pulled my ear to make sure I understood.

MYSTICS

Help me to find what I've lost,
If it was ever, however briefly, mine,
You who may have found it.
Old man praying in the privy,
Lonely child drawing a secret room
And in it a stopped clock.

Seek to convey its truth to me
By hints and omens.
The room in shadow, perhaps the wrong room?
The cockroach on the wall,
The naked lovers kissing
On the TV with the sound off.
I could hear the red faucet drip.

Or else restore to plain view
What is eternally invisible
And speaks by being silent.
Blue distances to the North,
The fires of the evening to the West,
Christ himself in pain, panhandling
On the altar of the storefront church
With a long bloody nail in each palm.

In this moment of amazement...
Since I do ask for it humbly,
Without greed, out of true need.
My teeth chattered so loudly,
My old dog got up to see what's the matter.
Oh divine lassitude, long drawn-out sigh
As the vision came and went.

VIA DEL TRITONE

In Rome, on the street of that name,
I was walking alone in the sun
In the noonday heat, when I saw a house
With shutters closed, the sight of which
Pained me so much, I could have
Been born there and left inconsolably.

The ochre walls, the battered old door
I was tempted to push open and didn't,
Knowing already the coolness of the entrance,
The garden with a palm tree beyond,
And the dark stairs on the left.

Shutters closed to cool shadowy rooms
With impossibly high ceilings,
And here and there a watery mirror
And my pale and contorted face
To greet me and startle me again and again.

"You found what you were looking for,"
I expected someone to whisper.
But there was no one, neither there
Nor in the street, which was deserted
In that monstrous heat that gives birth
To false memories and tritons.

THE SECRET

I have my excuse, Mr. Death,
The old note my mother wrote
The day I missed school.
Snow fell. I told her my head hurt
And my chest. The clock struck
The hour. I lay in my father's bed
Pretending to be asleep.

Through the windows I could see
The snow-covered roofs. In my mind
I rode a horse; I was in a ship
On a stormy sea. Then I dozed off.
When I woke, the house was still.
Where was my mother?
Had she written the note and left?

I rose and went searching for her.
In the kitchen our white cat sat
Picking at the bloody head of a fish.
In the bathroom the tub was full,
The mirror and the window fogged over.

When I wiped them, I saw my mother
In her red bathrobe and slippers
Talking to a soldier on the street
While the snow went on falling
And she put a finger
To her lips, and held it there.

From *Walking the Black Cat,* 1996

MIRRORS AT 4 A.M.

You must come to them sideways
In rooms webbed in shadow,
Sneak a view of their emptiness
Without them catching
A glimpse of you in return.

The secret is,
Even the empty bed is a burden to them,
A pretense.
They are more themselves keeping
The company of a blank wall,
The company of time and eternity

Which, begging your pardon,
Cast no image
As they admire themselves in the mirror,
While you stand to the side
Pulling a hanky out
To wipe your brow surreptitiously.

CAMEO APPEARANCE

I had a small, nonspeaking part
In a bloody epic. I was one of the
Bombed and fleeing humanity.
In the distance our great leader
Crowed like a rooster from a balcony,
Or was it a great actor
Impersonating our great leader?

That's me there, I said to the kiddies.
I'm squeezed between the man
With two bandaged hands raised
And the old woman with her mouth open
As if she were showing us a tooth

That hurts badly. The hundred times
I rewound the tape, not once
Could they catch sight of me
In that huge gray crowd,
That was like any other gray crowd.

Trot off to bed, I said finally.
I know I was there. One take
Is all they had time for.
We ran, and the planes grazed our hair,
And then they were no more
As we stood dazed in the burning city,
But, of course, they didn't film that.

WHAT THE GYPSIES TOLD MY GRANDMOTHER WHILE SHE WAS STILL A YOUNG GIRL

War, illness and famine will make you their favorite grandchild.
You'll be like a blind person watching a silent movie.
You'll chop onions and pieces of your heart
    into the same hot skillet.
Your children will sleep in a suitcase tied with a rope.
Your husband will kiss your breasts every night
    as if they were two gravestones.

Already the crows are grooming themselves
    for you and your people.
Your oldest son will lie with flies on his lips
    without smiling or lifting his hand.
You'll envy every ant you meet in your life
    and every roadside weed.
Your body and soul will sit on separate stoops
    chewing the same piece of gum.

Little cutie, are you for sale? the devil will say.
The undertaker will buy a toy for your grandson.
Your mind will be a hornet's nest even on your
    deathbed.
You will pray to God but God will hang a sign
    that He's not to be disturbed.
Question no further, that's all I know.

LITTLE UNWRITTEN BOOK

Rocky was a regular guy, a loyal friend.
The trouble was he was only a cat.
Let's practice, he'd say, and he'd pounce
On his shadow on the wall.
I have to admit, I didn't learn a thing.
I often sat watching him sleep.
If the birds tried to have a bit of fun in the yard,
He opened one eye.
I even commended him for good behavior.

He was black except for the white gloves he wore.
He played the piano in the parlor
By walking over its keys back and forth.
With exquisite tact he chewed my ear
If I wouldn't get up from my chair.
Then one day he vanished. I called.
I poked in the bushes.
I walked far into the woods.

The mornings were the hardest. I'd put out
A saucer of milk at the back door.
Peekaboo, a bird called out. She knew.
At one time we had ten farmhands working for us.
I'd make a megaphone with my hands and call.
I still do, though it's been years.
Rocky, I cry!
And now the bird is silent too.

SLAUGHTERHOUSE FLIES

Evenings, they ran their bloody feet
Over the pages of my schoolbooks.
With eyes closed, I can still hear
The trees on our street
Saying their moody farewell to summer,

And someone at home recalling
The weary old cows, hesitating,
At long last growing suspicious
Just as the blade drops down on them.

AN ADDRESS WITH EXCLAMATION POINTS

I accused History of gluttony;
Happiness of anorexia!

O History, cruel and mystical,
You ate Russia as if it were
A pot of white beans cooked with
Sausage, smoked ribs and ham hocks!

O Happiness, whose every miserly second
Is brimming with eternity!
You sat over a dish of vanilla custard
Without ever touching it!

The silent heavens were peeved!
They made the fair skies at sunset
Flash their teeth and burp from time to time,
Till our wedding picture slid off the wall.

The kitchen is closed, the waiters shouted!
No more vineyard snails in garlic butter!
No more ox tripe fried in onions!
We have only tears of happiness left!

ENTERTAINING THE CANARY

Yellow feathers,
Is it true
You chirp to the cop
On the beat?

Desist. Turn your
Nervous gaze
At the open bathroom door
Where I'm soaping

My love's back
And putting my chin on her shoulder
So I can do the same for her
Breasts and crotch.

Sing. Flutter your wings
As if you were applauding,
Or I'll throw her black slip
Over your gilded cage.

GHOSTS

It's Mr. Brown looking much better
Than he did in the morgue.
He's brought me a huge carp
In a bloodstained newspaper.
What an odd visit.
I haven't thought of him in years.

Linda is with him and so is Sue.
Two pale and elegant fading memories
Holding each other by the hand.
Even their lipstick is fresh
Despite all the scientific proofs
To the contrary.

Is Linda going to cook the fish?
She turns and gazes in the direction
Of the kitchen while Sue
Continues to watch me mournfully.
I don't believe any of it,
And still I'm scared stiff.

I know of no way to respond,
So I do nothing.
The windows are open. The air's thick
With the scent of magnolias.
Drops of evening rain are dripping
From the dark and heavy leaves.
I take a deep breath; I close my eyes.

Dear specters, I don't even believe
You are here, so how is it
You're making me comprehend
Things I would rather not know just yet?

It's the way you stare past me
At what must already be my own ghost,
Before taking your leave,
As unexpectedly as you came in,
Without one of us breaking the silence.

AT THE COOKOUT

The wives of my friends
Have the air
Of having shared a secret.
Their eyes are lowered
But when we ask them
Why
They only glance at each other
And smile,
Which only increases our desire
To know . . .

Something they did
Long ago,
Heedless of the consequences,
That left
Such a lingering sweetness?

Is that the explanation
For the way
They rest their chins
In the palms of their hands,
Their eyes closed
In the summer heat?

Come tell us,
Or give us a hint.
Trace a word or just a single letter
In the wine
Spilled on the table.

No reply. Both of them
Lovey-dovey
With the waning sunlight
And the evening breeze
On their faces.

The husbands drinking
And saying nothing,
Dazed and mystified as they are
By their wives' power
To give
And take away happiness,
As if their heads
Were crawling with snakes.

CLUB MIDNIGHT

Are you the sole owner of a seedy nightclub?

Are you its sole customer, sole bartender,
Sole waiter prowling around the empty tables?

Do you put on wee-hour girlie shows
With dead stars of black-and-white films?

Is your office upstairs over the neon lights,
Or down deep in the rat cellar?

Are bearded Russian thinkers your silent partners?
Do you have a doorman by the name of Dostoyevsky?

Is Fu Manchu coming tonight?
Is Miss Emily Dickinson?

Do you happen to have an immortal soul?
Do you have a sneaky suspicion that you have none?

Is that why you flip a white pair of dice,
In the dark, long after the joint closes?

PASTORAL HARPSICHORD

A house with a screened-in porch
On the road to nowhere.
The missus topless because of the heat,
A bag of Frito Banditos in her lap.
President Bush on TV
Watching her every bite.

Poor reception, that's the one
Advantage we have here,
I said to the mutt lying at my feet
And sighing in sympathy.
On another channel the preacher
Came chaperoned by his ghost
When he shut his eyes full of tears
To pray for dollars.

"Bring me another beer," I said to her ladyship,
And when she wouldn't oblige,
I went out to make chamber music
Against the sunflowers in the yard.

HAVE YOU MET MISS JONES?

I have. At a funeral
Pulling down her skirt to cover her knees
While inadvertently
Showing us her cleavage
Down to the tips of her nipples.

A stranger, wobbly on her heels,
Negotiating the exit
While the assembled mourners
Watched her rear end
With visible interest.

Presidential hopefuls
Will continue to lie to the American people
As we sit here bereaved.
New hatred will sweep the globe
Faster than hurricanes.
Sewer rats will sniff around
Lit cash machines
While her beauty lives on.

Miss Jones, you'll be safe
With the insomniacs, toasted
Where they pour wine from a bottle
Wrapped in a white napkin,
Eat lamb sausage with pan-fried potatoes,
And grow misty-eyed recalling

The way you trotted past the open coffin,
Past our dear friend
Starting his long siesta.
A cute little number an old man said,
But who was she?
Miss Jones, the guest book told us.

From *Jackstraws*, 1999

THE SOUL HAS MANY BRIDES

In India I was greatly taken up
With a fly in a temple
Which gave me the distinct feeling
It was possible, just possible,
That we had met before.

Was it in Mexico City?
Climbing the blood-spotted, yellow legs
Of the crucified Christ
While his eyes grew larger and larger.
"May God seat you on the highest throne
Of his invisible Kingdom,"
A blind beggar said to me in English.
He knew what I saw.

At the saloon where Pancho Villa
Fired his revolvers at the ceiling,
On the bare ass of a naked nymph
Stepping out of a lake in a painting,
And now shamelessly crawling up
One of Buddha's nostrils,
Whose smile got even more secretive,
Even more squint-eyed.

MUMMY'S CURSE

Befriending an eccentric young woman,
The sole resident of a secluded Victorian mansion.
She takes long walks in the evening rain,
And so do I, with my hair full of dead leaves.

In her former life, she was an opera singer.
She remembers the rich Neapolitan pastries,
Points to a bit of fresh whipped cream
Still left in the corner of her lower lip,
Tells me she dragged a wooden cross once
Through a leper town somewhere in India.

I was born in Copenhagen, I confide in turn.
My father was a successful mortician.
My mother never lifted her nose out of a book.
Arthur Schopenhauer ruined our happy home.
Since then, a day doesn't go by without me
Sticking a loaded revolver inside my mouth.

She had walked ahead of me and had turned
Like a lion tamer, towering with a whip in hand.
Luckily, in that moment, the mummy sped by
On a bicycle carrying someone's pizza order
And cursing the mist and the potholes.

THE COMMON INSECTS OF NORTH AMERICA

Bumble Bee, Soldier Bug, Mormon Cricket,
They are all out there somewhere
Behind Joe's Garage, in the tall weeds
By the snake handlers's church,
On the fringe of a beaver pond.

Painted Beauty is barefoot and wears shades.
Clouded Wood Nymph has been sight-seeing
And has caught a shiver. Book Louse
Is reading about the battle of Gettysburg.
Chinese Mantid has climbed a leaf to pray again.

Hermit Beetle and Rat Flea are feeling amorous
And are going to a drive-in movie.
Widow Dragonfly doing splits in the yard
Could use some serious talking to by her children
Before she comes to a tragic end.

THE TOY

The brightly painted horse
Had a boy's face,
And four small wheels
Under his feet,

Plus a long string
To pull him this way and that
Across the floor,
Should you care to.

A string in-waiting
That slipped away
With many wiles
From each and every try.

★

Knock and they'll answer,
My mother told me,
So I climbed the four flights
And went in unannounced.

And found the small toy horse
For the taking

In the ensuing emptiness
And the fading daylight
That still gives me a shudder
As if I held in my hand
The key to mysteries.

Where is the Lost and Found
And the quiet entry,
The undeveloped film
Of the few clear moments
Of our blurred lives.

Where's the drop of blood
And the tiny nail
That pricked my finger
As I bent down to touch the toy,
And caught its eye?

*

Wintry light,
My memories are
Steep stairwells
In dusty buildings
On dead-end streets,

Where I talk to the walls
And closed doors
As if they understood me.

The wooden toy sitting pretty.

No, quieter than that.

Like the sound of eyebrows
Raised by a villain
In a silent movie.

Psst, someone said behind my back.

From *Night Picnic,* 2001

UNMADE BEDS

They like shady rooms,
Peeling wallpaper,
Cracks on the ceiling,
Flies on the pillow.

If you are tempted to lie down,
Don't be surprised,
You won't mind the dirty sheets,
The rasp of rusty springs
As you make yourself comfy.
The room is a darkened movie theater
Where a grainy,
Black-and-white film is being shown.

A blur of disrobed bodies
In the moment of sweet indolence
That follows lovemaking,
When the meanest of hearts
Comes to believe
Happiness can last forever.

THE ONE TO WORRY ABOUT

I failed miserably at imagining nothing.
Something always came to keep me company:
A small nameless bug crossing the table,
The memory of my mother, the ringing in my ear.
I was distracted and perplexed.
A hole is invariably a hole in something.

About seven this morning, a lone beggar
Waited for me with his small, sickly dog,
Whose eyes grew bigger on seeing me.
There goes, the eyes said, that nice man
To whom (appearances to the contrary)
Nothing in this whole wide world is sacred.

I was still a trifle upset entering the bakery
When an unknown woman stepped out
Of the back to wait on me dressed for a night
On the town in a low-cut, tight-fitting black dress.
Her face was solemn, her eyes averted,
While she placed a muffin in my hand,
As if all along she knew what I was thinking.

SUNDAY PAPERS

The butchery of the innocent
Never stops. That's about all
We can ever be sure of, love,
Even more sure than of this roast
You are bringing out of the oven.

It's Sunday. The congregation
Files slowly out of the church
Across the street. A good many
Carry Bibles in their hands.
It's the vague desire for truth
And the mighty fear of it
That makes them turn up
Despite the glorious spring weather.

In the hallway, the old mutt
Just now had the honesty
To growl at his own image in the mirror,
Before lumbering off to the kitchen
Where the lamb roast sat
In your outstretched hands
Smelling of garlic and rosemary.

THE ALTAR

The plastic statue of the Virgin
On top of a bedroom dresser
With a blackened mirror
From a bad-dream grooming salon.

Two pebbles from the grave of a rock star,
A small, grinning windup monkey,
A bronze Egyptian coin
And a red movie-ticket stub.

A splotch of sunlight on the framed
Communion photograph of a boy
With the eyes of someone
Who will drown in a lake real soon.

An altar dignifying the god of chance.
What is beautiful, it cautions,
Is found accidentally and not sought after.
What is beautiful is easily lost.

MY FATHER ATTRIBUTED IMMORTALITY TO WAITERS

for Derek Walcott

For surely, there's no difficulty in understanding
The unreality of an occasional customer
Such as ourselves seated at one of the many tables
As pale as the cloth that covers them.

Time in its augmentations and diminutions
Does not concern these two in the least.
They stand side by side facing the street,
Wearing identical white jackets and fixed smiles,

Ready to incline their heads in welcome
Should one of us come through the door
After reading the high-priced menu on this street
Of many hunched figures and raised collars.

THE LIVES OF THE ALCHEMISTS

The great labor was always to efface oneself,
Reappear as something entirely different:
The pillow of a young woman in love,
A ball of lint pretending to be a spider.

Black boredoms of rainy country nights
Thumbing the writings of illustrious adepts
Offering advice on how to proceed with the transmutation
Of a figment of time into eternity.
The true master, one of them counseled,
Needs a hundred years to perfect his art.

In the meantime, the small arcana of the frying pan,
The smell of olive oil and garlic wafting
From room to empty room, the black cat
Rubbing herself against your bare leg
While you shuffle toward the distant light
And the tinkle of glasses in the kitchen.

From *The Voice at 3:00 A.M.*, 2003

GRAYHEADED SCHOOLCHILDREN

Old men have bad dreams,
So they sleep little.
They walk on bare feet
Without turning on the light,
Or they stand leaning
On gloomy furniture
Listening to their hearts beat.

The one window across the room
Is black like a blackboard.
Every old man is alone
In this classroom, squinting
At that fine chalk line
That divides being-here
From being-here-no-more.

No matter. It was a glass of water
They were going to get,
But not just yet.
They listen for mice in the walls,
A car passing on the street,
Their dead fathers shuffling past them
On their way to the kitchen.

SERVING TIME

Another dreary day in time's invisible
Penitentiary, making license plates
With lots of zeros, walking lockstep counter-
Clockwise in the exercise yard or watching
The lights dim when some poor fellow,
Who could as well be me, gets fried.

Here on death row, I read a lot of books.
First it was law, as you'd expect.
Then came history, ancient and modern.
Finally philosophy—all that being and nothingness stuff.
The more I read, the less I understand.
Still, other inmates call me professor.

Did I mention that we had no guards?
It's a closed book who locks
And unlocks the cell doors for us.
Even the executions we carry out
By ourselves, attaching the wires,
Playing warden, playing chaplain

All because a little voice in our head
Whispers something about our last appeal
Being denied by God himself.
The others hear nothing, of course,
But that, typically, you may as well face it,
Is how time runs things around here.

LATE SEPTEMBER

The mail truck goes down the coast
Carrying a single letter.
At the end of a long pier
The bored seagull lifts a leg now and then
And forgets to put it down.
There is a menace in the air
Of tragedies in the making.

Last night you thought you heard television
In the house next door.
You were sure it was some new
Horror they were reporting,
So you went out to find out.
Barefoot, wearing just shorts.
It was only the sea sounding weary
After so many lifetimes
Of pretending to be rushing off somewhere
And never getting anywhere.

This morning, it felt like Sunday.
The heavens did their part
By casting no shadow along the boardwalk
Or the row of vacant cottages,
Among them a small church
With a dozen gray tombstones huddled close
As if they, too, had the shivers.

From *My Noiseless Entourage*, 2005

SELF-PORTRAIT IN BED

For imaginary visitors, I had a chair
Made of cane I found in the trash.
There was a hole where its seat was
And its legs were wobbly
But it still gave a dignified appearance.

I myself never sat in it, though
With the help of a pillow one could do that
Carefully, with knees drawn together
The way she did once,
Leaning back to laugh at her discomfort.

The lamp on the night table
Did what it could to bestow
An air of mystery to the room.
There was a mirror, too, that made
Everything waver as in a fishbowl

If I happened to look that way,
Red-nosed, about to sneeze,
With a thick wool cap pulled over my ears,
Reading some Russian in bed,
Worrying about my soul, I'm sure.

TO DREAMS

I'm still living at all the old addresses,
Wearing dark glasses even indoors,
On the hush-hush sharing my bed
With phantoms, visiting the kitchen

After midnight to check the faucet.
I'm late for school, and when I get there
No one seems to recognize me.
I sit disowned, sequestered and withdrawn.

These small shops open only at night
Where I make my unobtrusive purchases,
These backdoor movie houses in seedy neighborhoods
Still showing grainy films of my life.

The hero always full of extravagant hope
Losing it all in the end?—whatever it was—
Then walking out into the cold, disbelieving light
Waiting close-lipped at the exit.

MY NOISELESS ENTOURAGE

We were never formally introduced.
I had no idea of their number.
It was like a discreet entourage
Of homegrown angels and demons
All of whom I had met before
And had since largely forgotten.

In time of danger, they made themselves scarce.
Where did they all vanish to?
I asked some felon one night
While he held a knife to my throat,
But he was spooked too,
Letting me go without a word.

It was disconcerting, downright frightening
To be reminded of one's solitude,
Like opening a children's book—
With nothing better to do—reading about stars,
How they can afford to spend centuries
Traveling our way on a glint of light.

DESCRIPTION OF A LOST THING

It never had a name,
Nor do I remember how I found it.
I carried it in my pocket
Like a lost button
Except it wasn't a button.

Horror movies,
All-night cafeterias,
Dark barrooms
And pool halls,
On rain-slicked streets.

It led a quiet, unremarkable existence
Like a shadow in a dream,
An angel on a pin,
And then it vanished.
The years passed with their row

Of nameless stations,
Till somebody told me *this is it*!
And fool that I was,
I got off on an empty platform
With no town in sight.

MY TURN TO CONFESS

A dog trying to write a poem on why he barks,
That's me, dear reader!
They were about to kick me out of the library
But I warned them,
My master is invisible and all-powerful.
Still, they kept dragging me out by the tail.

In the park the birds spoke freely of their own vexations.
On a bench, I saw an old woman
Cutting her white curly hair with imaginary scissors
While staring into a small pocket mirror.

I didn't say anything then,
But that night I lay slumped on the floor,
Chewing on a pencil,
Sighing from time to time,
Growling, too, at something out there
I could not bring myself to name.

IN THE PLANETARIUM

Never-yet-equaled, wide-screen blockbuster
That grew more and more muddled
After a spectacular opening shot.
The pace, even for the most patient
Killingly slow despite the promise
Of a show-stopping, eye-popping ending:
The sudden shriveling of the whole
To its teensy starting point, erasing all—
Including this bag of popcorn we are sharing.

Yes, an intriguing but finally irritating
Puzzle with no answer forthcoming tonight
From the large cast of stars and galaxies
In what may be called a prodigious
Expenditure of time, money and talent.
"Let's get the fuck out of here," I said
Just as her upraised eyes grew moist
And she confided to me, much too loudly,
"I have never seen anything so beautiful."

PIGEONS AT DAWN

Extraordinary efforts are being made
To hide things from us, my friend.
Some stay up into the wee hours
To search their souls.
Others undress each other in darkened rooms.

The creaky old elevator
Took us down to the icy cellar first
To show us a mop and a bucket
Before it deigned to ascend again
With a sigh of exasperation.

Under the vast, early-dawn sky
The city lay silent before us.
Everything on hold:
Rooftops and water towers,
Clouds and wisps of white smoke.

We must be patient, we told ourselves,
See if the pigeons will coo now
For the one who comes to her window
To feed them angel cake,
All but invisible, but for her slender arm.